Are We Ape or Angel?

According to evolutionists we are from the ape family of animals. They look only on the physical plane. On the mental and intellectual plane, there is a vast difference that evolutionists can't explain. We are vastly superior in knowledge, understanding, insight and capabilities. And when it comes to spiritual matters, there is no comparison!

What are we? Where are we from? Why were we created? What purpose does God have in mind? There is a fantastic future that God has prepared for us! It is beyond the wildest dream of the average religious person!

Learn about your incredible potential!

Pieter Voges

Are We Ape or Angel?

Disclaimer

© 2023, Author P. Voges

This Book is designed to provide information and motivation to our readers. It may contain links to other websites or content belonging to or originating from third parties or links to websites and features. Such external links are not investigated, monitored, or checked for accuracy, adequacy, validity, reliability, availability or completeness.

All information in this Book is provided in good faith, however we make no representation or warranty of any kind, express or implied, regarding the accuracy, adequacy, validity, reliability, availability, or completeness of any information.

All rights reserved. Except for brief excerpts for review purposes, no
part of this publication may be reproduced or used in any form or by any means—electronic or mechanical, including photocopying, recording, or information storage and retrieval systems.

Contents

Introduction

Paleontologists look at bone fractures and fossil records of humanoids, and make some assumptions. They fill in gaps with sculpture, and complete their ideas. They imagine flesh on the bones, and assign a skin color that agrees with their assumptions. Then they imagine that the body that they presume that existed long ago had a mind like ours. They even assume that their humanoid image that they assembled can speak! But they have never found writings and books from their humanoids, neither any evidence that their humanoids could communicate in complex concepts. And did their humanoids have any religion? Did they worship God?

On the physical plain there are some commonality between us and those humanoids, but there are also many differences. A tweak in the DNA can result in quite a difference in a grown being. And a little tweak in DNA can result in hands and feet that are clearly made for different purposes.

On the intellectual plain there are vast differences. Our ability to plan ahead, plant food, calculate seasons, gather and store water for future use, and establish cities are vastly superior. In fact, it is non-existing among the ape species! Have any ape ever spoke a word? Have they written any material ever? Have they ever tried to and succeeded in reading books?

On the religious front, they are totally cut off from having the faintest knowledge of God! Unfortunately, so are some humans, but that is by choice, rather than created capability.

The more we think about it, the more we have to agree that humans are a totally different species, a totally different design. And the only way to logically explain the vast difference is to acknowledge that there is a Creator that designed this vast difference.

And then we come to the all-important question – why are we so different? Why have God created us? Why do we exist? What was the purpose in creating us with such vast potential? And what is the total potential that God had – and still has – in mind for us?

We will investigate all of that, using your Bible, and it may be different than what is commonly assumed. The atheists and paleontologists may have blurred the picture for most people. And then the apostasy and partial reform that started in the 16th century also muddied the understanding.

First, we can consider problems with the theory of macro evolution.

Secondly, we will investigate the early creation of Angels.

Then we will look at the rebellion of some of them, and resultant destruction in the universe.

We can then consider God's Plan with the renewal of the surface of the earth, and the special creation of humankind, and unfortunate fall from grace.

But God knew that was possible, and His plan of redemption is active. Do we fully understand that plan?

Ultimately some will be saved, and be resurrected into eternal life to serve God. What will that life be? What will we do?

The final redemption of some humans and Angels is the ultimate goal, and the universe will rejoice. Finally mankind will also become a multi planetary species!

1 Scientific Assumptions

Palaeontologists suggest that humans evolved from apes. The atheistic dogma is based on theory, which they postulate to be factual. However, it leaves a lot of questions unanswered. If we are to assume that humans evolved from apes, these concerns must be addressed. In this chapter we will raise these concerns. Clear scientific prove on these issues are lacking. There is not clearly documented evidence, but mainly theory. After all, nobody lived for millions of years to have seen macro evolution happen, let alone document the process. So, firstly, let's consider these concerns in the light of Biblical guidance.

~~~~~

The earth is unique

The Bible shows that the earth is unique in the universe. Scientists are trying, by all means, to find any inkling of life anywhere else in the universe. Probes and rovers have been sent to other planets. Massive antennas listen for any sign of an intelligent radio wave from outer space. Not a single sign of any intelligence have been found. If we as capable humans are the result of such an infinitesimally small chance of having happened by chance, surely there should have been evidence by now. Surely the change of life elsewhere could have been bigger at other planets! But so far, there has been nothing whatsoever.

Rovers on Mars have shown that water once flowed on Mars! All the ingredients of biological life existed on
~~~~~

Mars! Yet no evidence of one single cell has been found. If life on the earth formed by mere chance, why did it not form on Mars?

~~~~~

DNA survival

Quite a lot of complex processes are required to maintain DNA. DNA in a cell cannot survive in the cell without repair processes. There are over 100 human repair genes. Without these, the DNA in our cells will not survive. Even water destroys DNA. Cells need DNA to program their function in an organism to survive. Cells cannot form into functional life forms without the transfer of DNA information through messenger RNA. What came first, the cell or the DNA?

~~~~~

Natural selection

Natural variance designed into existing species allows adaptation to environmental changes—this rather preserved existing species. Yet we do not find interspecies migrations. For instance, cats are cats, and dogs are dogs. There is a huge amount of variance in the cat species, from the smallest house cat to the largest lion roaming on the continents. Yet they never interbred with dogs. Can science show us a cat/dog? Or can they accept that the Creator created DNA to allow variance, and hence preserve species in the face of changing environments, even climate change? What Darwin saw on the islands was merely adaptation allowed by God in the DNA of species. By the way, Darwin never knew of DNA. In his time, the microscope was not yet powerful enough to have discovered DNA. One wonders if he would have wanted to reconsider his book in the face of DNA evidence.

~~~~~

Speed of adaption

Evolution proposes that changes in species happened over millions of years. However, there is evidence to the contrary. Researchers have found that tiny stickleback fishes can adapt (evolve) from warmer lakes to cold fishponds in a matter of three generations. This took three years. They also migrated from seawater to freshwater within a few years! According to the theory of evolution, it should have taken millions of years. Prawns from a system of caves in South Africa were found to be completely blind. They had no eyes. Some were taken to a lab. They obviously multiplied in the lab. After a mere seven generations, they had fully functional eyes. According to the theory of evolution, it should have taken millions of years! There are many more such examples that throw the assumptions of the theory of evolution out of the lab window!

~~~~~

The eye

How did the eye evolve? At what stage and by what mechanism did a plant develop an eye? Why did the plant grow eyes? This is one of the most baffling proposals of the theory of evolution. Many articles have been written on this subject, but it is clearly not possible to evolve a plant into flesh and blood beings with eyes. Then we have to make the assumption that plants became animals at the same time, for the one can't exit without the other in the long term.

And when did plants decide to pick up roots and walk? Plants are clearly dependent on the ground in which they are rooted. Pull out any plant, and it dies. So the transition is clearly farfetched. It requires a leap of faith a million times more than believing the Word of God!

~~~~~

Superiority of humans

Evolution would have us assume we come from primates. But recent studies into the human DNA progression presented another barrier. We can see that as we produce offspring, the amount of DNA modification increases. If we assume the DNA strand can be stretched out in a line, the length of the section varied increases. This means we can work backward and arrive at the point where we have zero variance length. Surprisingly this amounted to only a few thousand years when it comes to humankind, and that individual was a woman. We can guess her name. Eve! And even more significantly, there is no continuance from any of the primates. Humankind's DNA seems to have started somewhere, uniquely. This is what was stated in science documentation.

But even more incredible is Mankind's ability to communicate. In Genesis, God asked Adam to begin
~~~~~

naming things. There is much more to this. Humanity was given a spirit in a small way like God has a Holy Spirit, and it gives Mankind the ability to comprehend abstract spiritual concepts such as love and faith, Mankind is a massive leap higher than animals, any animal. By the extrapolation of the theory of evolution, we should not be more than the primates, yet we developed computers, went to the moon and back, and is testing the universe for signs of life! We have achieved a million times more than the primates within a few thousand years! Yet primates are stagnant. If we are from the primates, why did they not develop like we? Evolution cannot explain this.

~~~~~

Probability of cells

Knowing what we know today of cells and particularly the DNA required to program them, the probability of molecules getting together by chance and forming a cell with DNA and all supporting structures is impossible.

According to the laws of probability, an event needs a chance of better than 1 in 10 to the power of 50. Remember that according to the evolutionist, the earth is about 3 to 5 billion years old, but the figure is adjusted regularly. We only have so much time and space. However, the chance of amino acids forming a protein is 4.9 in 10 to the power of 191. Then it cannot survive without supporting the maintenance mechanism. If it formed, it would have died quickly. Life mechanisms are very much interdependent on other life mechanisms.

Many studies on the probability of life happening by chance have been done, and it seems improbable. The
~~~~~

figures and statistics indicate that the universe is far too young for life to have happened randomly. Even if mathematicians can get the figures right, then it still does not prove that self-sustaining life formed randomly. According to statistics, we don't exist!

Even if the universe started with a big bang, what existed before? Still, we need a Creator. And the Bible does allow that possibility.

Even if the earth is 3 to 5 billion years old, self-sustaining life could not have happened within time and chance. There must have been a supernatural intelligent intervention. And the Bible does allow for the possibility of a fallen host of angels that did their own thing on the earth in the pre-historic world. There is Biblical support for the notion that the earth was plagued by catastrophic events, which will be repeated again. The fossil record does allow Biblical interpretation.

Even if species adapt to changing environmental issues, the Bible does allow for this to be the case. Surely God did program adaptability into the DNA and genes of species. However, there cannot be change right across species. Evolutionists may find it difficult to accept the reality of all these missing links.

Humanity is a unique species with mental capabilities well beyond the primates. Our DNA does not reach back to the primates. If we look at the recent scientific evidence, we all have to accept that humanity is a recent creation, "in the image of God".

If we all take a step back from our assumptions that we based our beliefs on, and face the facts with an open mind, then we can meet halfway, without compromising science or Faith.

~~~~~
~~~~~

Leap of faith

Some scientists want us to believe their theories. They want us to believe a single cell formed by chance somewhere on the earth. Lately the theory is that single cells came with asteroids or comets traveling for billions of years frozen solid at minus 300 degrees or more, and yet lived again. They want us to believe this single cell somehow also had the ability to replicate. They want us to believe the cell became more complex by chance, and formed a plant. Then they want us to believe the plant at one stage decided to uproot itself and form feet that can walk. At the same time eyes had to form by chance else it would walk into objects and perhaps die.

So some scientists want us to take a leap of faith in their postulations. Have any of them lived for a thousand years? Have any of them lived for a million, or even better, a billions years? Have they actually observed evolution from sand organisms to animals that they can be so sure of it that they can say the Bible is nothing but myths? If they want to prove that there is no God that intervened at times to bring forth a creation that will raise mankind who can reach out to Him and attain eternal life, it is a sad day. Many accept through their theories that there is no God. Hence they accept defeat and death.

If we have a choice to have faith in the Bible or some scientific theories, who would you prefer? In the end it is a matter of faith. Both options require faith. But for a few real serious Christians it has gone beyond faith into a surety that comes from life in the presence of a miracle working God.

The author can attest to how many times he was saved from deadly car accidents, and even near plane incidents, and poisonous snakes and plants. If it was only left to chance he should have been dead by now. If there was no God, these books would not have been written.

One of the biggest scientists that walked the earth was Einstein. Yet in all his wisdom he never doubted God. All the science did not persuade him to doubt the scriptures. Rather, it strengthened his faith.

Since some scientists want to nullify the God of the Bible, we must consider all the evidence in a court of law, where some people want to execute the Creator. Consider such a case before a court of law in a civilised world, where reason prevails.

What witnesses will these people bring against the Creator? Bones? Ash? Rocks? They will expect the judge to view that against clearly written testimony proven thousands years ago through the fulfilment of prophecy. Such very flimsy circumstantial evidence from some scientists will never even be considered before a reasonable judge. The case will be thrown out even before the court date! Yet some are keen to accept it, and so seal their fate in the Judgment Day. They destroy the faith of many, and so commit spiritual murder. May God have mercy on their souls!

~~~~~

Are we from apes?

Paleontologists and biologists in many higher education institutions are assuming that humankind evolved from apes. In so doing they are destroying the Faith of many people. They may be committing spiritual abortion!

We need to set some defining arguments immediately.
~~~~~

There is macroevolution and microevolution. Macroevolution suggests that all life came from single cell organisms that spontaneously gained higher intelligent life forms, to eventually evolve to the ultimate life form – you and me. They deny a all-knowing Creator. For them, you came from apes.

Then there is microevolution that suggests that species can evolve to adapt to circumstances, such as climate change, different food availability, survival challenges and major temperature differences. The suggestion is that God created adaptability in species.

In this chapter we will deal with the assumptions of macroevolution. Are you from apes?

There are several serious problems with the theory of macroevolution! We should discuss this now to show the glaring flaws with this godless doctrine.

Are We Ape or Angel?

2 In the beginning

The physical beginning of Genesis One is not the spiritual beginning. The spiritual beginning is shown by the apostle John. We will look at that, using the sacred names, so that we can also see that it is not really a Trinitarian statement. This is important for readers to really grasp the enormity of what is being discussed in this book, and the enormous potential of humankind.

~~~~~

The Spiritual beginning

"In the beginning was the Word [Logos], and the Word [Logos] was with God [Elohin], and the Word [Logos] was God [El]. He was in the beginning with God. All things came into being through Him, and without Him not even one thing came into being that has come into being."

(John 1:1-3, MKJV)

[between brackets mine, from Sacred Names Bible]

The Word was not exactly the one and only God, as can be seen from the Sacred Names Bible. But He was and is the only begotten Son of God.
~~~~~

"No one has seen God at any time; the Only-begotten Son, who is in the bosom of the Father, He has declared Him."

(John 1:18, MKJV)

From this we have to understand the following:

Jesus, whom many people have seen, is therefore not the Elohim, the Most High God, the Father of all. He was the Christ, and proved obedience in the flesh, and was resurrected to eternal life, proving the potential for human beings. Jesus Christ is the Only-begotten Son of God. All other beings, including Angels, were created. In fact, even the Angels were created through Christ.

A comparison can be made on an earthly plane, even though it may be inadequate on many levels. For instance, Mr. Toyota created robotic servants containing some form of artificial intelligence to assist in creating vehicles, and even to assist in homes. But Mr. Toyota had a flesh and blood son that looks much like him, and shares the same attributes, intelligence, hope and purpose with his dad. All the creations of the dad were done through his son.

All things in the universe were created by God through His Only-begotten Son, even the Angels. The Angels were obviously created before the physical universe. They were created as caretakers of the universe. They were all supposed to carry on with the process of developing the Universe.

Of particular interest was the Earth, on which new life was created. It was a wonderful experience and opportunity the develop animals that would live off plants. Some would live in the seas, while others would fly through the air. They would have some intelligence, and it was fantastic to see how it all developed. It was like an environment where artificial intelligence was placed in these created beings, and then they could all watch and see how it all played out.

Notice how God put Job in his place concerning the greatness of God, and His creation that He perceived, ordered and managed.

> "Where were you when I laid the foundations of the earth? Tell if you have understanding! Who has set its measurements, for you know? Or who has stretched the line on it? On what are its bases sunk, or who cast its cornerstone, when the morning stars sang together and all the sons of God shouted for joy?
>
> (Job 38:4-7, MKJV)

They were supposed to be overseers, which would intervene at times to keep steering the development in the right direction, to fulfill God's purposed. But there was potential for disaster.

The Angels were all created beings. They were not fully eternal like God. They had a beginning. Even the highest of them were created by God through His Only-begotten Son. Even the Cherub that corrupted himself and became Satan is a created spirit being.

> "You were the anointed cherub that covers, and I had put you in the holy height of God where you were; you have walked up and down in the midst of the stones of fire. You were perfect in your ways from the day that you were created, until iniquity was found in you."
>
> (Ezekiel 28:14-15, MKJV)

Having placed high intelligence and insight into powerful creative beings always risk the potential for rebellion, and disaster. If the overseers would get selfish, and become rebellious, desiring to deviate from the original purpose, plans and designs, all harmony could be lost. Confrontations would happen somewhere along the line, and if unchecked, eventually there would be war and destruction. This risk was to some extent the nature of the potential.

For instance to allow unlimited potential, some free moral agency is also the tradeoff. Let's investigate the logic behind that. Some animals are born and then walk within a few hours. They seem to be born to walk. It is already in their body and mind. Using computer terms, we would say they are hard wired. Human beings are not. A baby is born rather helpless. It takes months before a baby successfully crawls, and up to a year before it walks. But it can relearn the meaning of feet and hand movements. After a year it learns to walk, something few animals can do. Within two years it can ride a tricycle. After three years it can master a bicycle. Some even ride a unicycle after six years. Then some learn to start and ride a motorbike by age ten. As a grown-up it can ride cars, trucks, excavators, forklifts, airplanes, jet fighters and motorboats. No animals can do that. The benefit is that the human is not hardwired to get up and walk in the first few hours after birth; hence it can learn many different functions of hand and feet movements.

Unfortunately the same hands can also stab a knife, or shoot a gun, or lately type a command on a guided missile system to destroy a city! The potential is great on both side of the moral tree. That is what freedom means. Free moral agency that comes with unlimited mental and spiritual capabilities also brings unlimited potential for destruction and death.

Mankind faces this dilemma. The Angels also faced this dilemma, and some made the wrong choices, as we will see later.

~~~~~

The physical beginning

God created the physical universe for the Angels to continue with the creative process. Life would have been formed on many planets. They type of life would depend on available material, environment, elements in oversupply, and long term sustainability.

From God's Throne energy went out into the universe that turned into matter as it sped out into the empty space of the universe. What God envisioned happened, and formed galaxies of suns, planets and moons. Somewhere in the universe many Exoplanets would exist on which the Angels could form life. All across the universe life would be formed everywhere.

Of particular interest was the earth. God would begin the process of forming life on earth as an example for the Angels.

> "For so says Jehovah the Creator of the heavens, He is God, forming the earth and making it; He makes it stand, not creating it empty, but forming it to be inhabited. I am Jehovah, and there is no other."

(Isaiah 45:18, MKJV)

However, seeing life on the early earth and the incredible potential was perhaps too much for some of the
~~~~~

Angels. They were supposed to learn, to do likewise on other Exoplanets, but envy crept in.

A very senior Cherub, a morning Star, who was there in the beginning, and was supposed to help build life on Exoplanets under God's directions, wanted to take over, and did things his way. He wanted to supplant the Most High God and take over life on the earth. He though he had better ideas, and would make huge destructive animals to take over life forms that God formed initially. He wanted to establish himself over all the angels, and so supplant the Most High God, and relegates Him to a mere benign state figure with no say in all matters.

The one who became Satan would even continue to have influence in mankind's affairs as far as they would not turn to God, but rather wanted all to exert power, and so falling for the satanic notions that they can be great themselves, but they would all fail dismally, eventually ruling over failed states, with people eventually resorting to war to survive. And so, without God's guidance, all the nation building efforts would go up in smoke one day.

"How you are fallen from the heavens, O shining star, son of the morning! How you are cut down to the ground, you who weakened the nations! For you have said in your heart, I will go up to the heavens, I will exalt my throne above the stars of God; I will also sit on the mount of the congregation, in the sides of the north. I will go up above the heights of the clouds; I will be like the Most High. Yet you shall be brought down to hell, to the sides of the Pit. Those who see you shall stare and closely watch you, saying, Is this the man who made the earth to tremble; who shook kingdoms; who made the world as a wilderness, and destroyed its cities; who did not open the house for his prisoners? All the kings of the nations, even all of them, lie in glory, every one in his own house. But you are cast out of your grave like a hateful branch, and like the clothing of those who are slain, thrust through with a sword, that go down to the stones of the pit; like a dead body trampled under foot. You shall not be joined with them in burial, because you ruined your land and killed your people; the seed of evildoers shall never be famous."

(Isaiah 14:12-20, MKJV)

This fallen morning star swayed a third of the angels to follow his devious plans.

In the book of Revelation is a section describing the plans and motivations of spirit personalities which planned the birth and life of Jesus Christ, and also the devil which would do his best to thwart that plan. It mentions that the devil previously drew a third of the angels to follow his selfish ways.

"And his tail drew the third part of the stars of heaven, and cast them onto the earth. And the dragon stood before the woman being about to bear, so that when she bears he might devour her child."

(Revelation 12:4, MKJV)

These fallen angels previously were to oversee the ancient creation, but rather than maintain God's purposes, decided to influence the reproductive processes, to form massive and destructive animals, forever tearing each other apart. These altered beasts fulfilled the evil motives of these fallen angels, who looked on at the destruction they wrought. Like today's kids who play for days in their destructive computer games, so these angels looked on, and probably enjoy the horror they unfold. The fallen angels were largely unaffected at the time, since they were never flesh and blood animals, that would personally experience the constant fear for their lives, and the enormous suffering of being torn apart alive!

Perhaps they couldn't wait to see if they could influence the procreative process. Altering the DNA and genes would make changes to the animals. The desire to make bigger animals that would overcome other animals would be a great experiment for them.

The Angels began to deviate from God's guidance. So God had to remove them from their positions of power and bound their powers. This happened long ago, even before the Flood, even before the Creation Week where the surface of the earth was renewed according to Psalms 104:30.

"For if God did not spare sinning angels, but thrust them down into Tartarus, and delivered them into chains of darkness, being reserved to judgment. And He did not spare the old world, but saved Noah the eighth one, a preacher of righteousness, bringing in the flood upon the world of the ungodly."

(2 Peter 2:4-5, MKJV)

Some of the angels even abandoned their responsibilities, leaving the creation without overseers, and allowing it to degenerate. Life was lost in many worlds.

"And those angels not having kept their first place, but having deserted their dwelling-place, He has kept in everlasting chains under darkness for the judgment of a great Day;"

(Jude1:6, MKJV)

Even before the renewal of the earth after the previous catastrophic abandonment when dinosaurs roamed the world, Satan had corrupted himself, and was in a position to confront and tempt Eve and Adam in paradise.

"You have been in Eden the garden of God; every precious stone was your covering, the ruby, topaz, and the diamond, the beryl, the onyx, and the jasper, the sapphire, the turquoise, and the emerald, and gold. The workmanship of your tambourines and of your flutes was prepared in you in the day that you were created. You were the anointed cherub that covers, and I had put you in the holy height of God where you were; you have walked up and down in the midst of the stones of fire. You were perfect in your ways from the day that you were created, until iniquity was found in you."

(Ezekiel 28:13-15, MKJV)

This sin of some of the angels had a devastating effect on early creation. Even in the previous world before Noah and the Flood, the experimentation of the angels led to huge animals. This was a huge problem for mankind, who lived in fear of these massive animals, who regularly would come and destroy what people were trying to build up.

Men also commune with fallen angels – something that is forbidden by God - to learn how to modify and create huge offspring. Some sons then grew to become as tall as ten to twelve feet. Their skeletons have been found by archeologists, and the evidence is there for all to see.

"And Jehovah said, My spirit shall not always strive with man, in his erring; he is flesh. Yet his days shall be a hundred and twenty years. There were giants in the earth in those days. And also after that, when the sons of God came in to the daughters of men, and they bore to them, they were mighty men who existed of old, men of renown. and Jehovah saw that the wickedness of man was great in the earth, and every imagination of the thoughts of his heart was only evil continually. And Jehovah repented that He had made man on the earth, and He was angry to His heart. And Jehovah said, I will destroy man whom I have created, from the face of the earth, both man, and beast, and the creeping thing, and the fowls of the air. For I repent that I have made them."

(Genesis 6:3-7, MKJV)

That generation died out during the Flood, but a remnant of the problem even existed when King David probably killed the last few giants, as they were evolved by demons to destroy God's plans for Israel. This is the result of the fallen angels, and the damage they caused.

God allowed the problem to exist even during the first two millenniums of mankind's existence, so that we have the evidence of what a big problem that was, and how other species were wiped out, and violence and death was the order of the day every day! We had to understand that God will allow such behavior and people to die, so that humankind can learn how bad Satan's ways are, and the evidence exist for us today.

God then went ahead with His plan to create a human being that would replace the fallen angels eventually. They would be physical, so that they can completely comprehend the plight of the animals when evil is allowed to flourish. But they would be able to speak, read and write. They would have a spirit that would comprehend God and His Spirit, and be able to learn from God, and establish God's Kingdom and ways.

It must have tormented the fallen angels to learn that God was planning to make a new humanoid that would ultimately replace them. Hence they would always seek ways to ruin the lived and development of these humans, to block the way for them to attain eternal life and rule over the creation, to succeed where the fallen angels failed.

God then started the renewal of the surface of the earth.

"You send forth Your Spirit, they are created; and You renew the face of the earth."

(Psalms 104:30, MKJV)

The human beginning

God would make a new start. The fallen angels were limited in their capabilities, but would be given some leeway, so that mankind would learn and understand the results of not following God and His Son in their ways of peace. He would redo the animal creation, so that mankind can survive, but also understand the fear for life. Mankind would be half ape, but also half Angel with a tremendous potential. Mankind would learn compassion for the animals, but also develop Godly understanding, and have the incredible potential to one day live forever among the angels.

A new beginning was planned, and happened nearly 6000 years ago. The surface of the earth would be renewed. After the previous catastrophic life extinction event that God allowed, there would be a new beginning.

3 Genesis

God is about to begin the next phase of His creative plan. The earth would be renewed, and made habitable by a very unique creature. This creature would be like the animals, and live off the land, eating plants, but would also be like the Angels, capable to understand godly things. If this being would follow God's ways, they would see immediate positive results. If they disregard God, and follow their own shortsighted ideas, evil would come, and they would see a rapid deterioration in their situation. It would not take thousands of years to see the horrible end result. They will learn quite soon that God was right, and His ways are best. They would experience the pain in their own bodies. They would learn compassion on the animal kingdom.

> "And God said, Let Us make man in Our image, after Our likeness. And let them have dominion over the fish of the sea, and over the fowl of the heavens, and over the cattle, and over all the earth, and over all the creepers creeping on the earth. And God created man in His image; in the image of God He created him. He created them male and female."

(Genesis 1:26-27, MKJV)

Spiritually these humans would be able to comprehend God. They would be able to relate to God, just as the Angels are able to. And with superior intelligence, they would be able to rule over the animal kingdom. They would be able to plan ahead, provide food security, and feed the animals. So just on this physical plane of the animal kingdom, mankind has been given powers that far succeed that of any animal. We can monitor and predict the season's years ahead. We can form dams, and drill for water, and have windmills suck up water and continually provide water in the driest of places for people and animals.

> "And God blessed them. And God said to them, Be
> fruitful, and multiply and fill the earth, and subdue it.
> And have dominion over the fish of the sea and over the
> fowl of the heavens, and all animals that move upon the
> earth."

(Genesis 1:28, MKJV)

God gave mankind a head start, planting a garden for them, and began to educate them in good diet.

> "And Jehovah God formed man of the dust of the
> ground, and breathed into his nostrils the breath of life;
> and man became a living soul.

> And Jehovah God planted a garden eastward in Eden.
> And there He put the man whom He had formed.

Mankind was both like an animal, but also unique in that they would also be somewhat like the Angels. They would have a spirit with capabilities far above the animals.

> "But a spirit is in man giving them perception, even the
> breath of the Almighty."

(Job 32:8, MKJV)

The Spirit of God can unite with the human spirit to give understanding and insights into the Word of God, thereby developing faith in the Bible. This leads to conversion, repentance and thinking like the Angels.

Mankind may die like animals, and our breath eventually fails. But there is a spirit that God can gather and preserve for the resurrection.

> "For that which happens to the sons of men also happens to beasts, even one thing happens to them. As this one dies, so that one dies; yea, they all have one breath; so that a man has no advantage over a beast; for all is vanity. All go to one place; all are of the dust, and all return to dust again. Who knows the spirit of man that goes upward, and the spirit of the beast that goes downward?"

(Ecclesiastes 3:19-21, MKJV)

God can preserve the spirit of humankind for a later event, when some will be resurrected to eternal life, but other to further training and judgment.

> "But if the Spirit of the One who raised up Jesus from the dead dwells in you, the One who raised up Christ from the dead shall also make your mortal bodies alive by His Spirit who dwells in you."

(Romans 8:11, MKJV)

There is a great difference between humankind, and the rest of the animal kingdom!

However, humans will have to prove their loyalty to God. Just like the Angels had to choose whether they will follow God's plan, or go off and try their own ideas, and rebel against God, so humankind also have that power of choice, and with that freedom and power comes consequences.

> And out of the ground Jehovah God caused to grow every tree that is pleasant to the sight, and good for food. The tree of life also was in the middle of the garden, and the tree of knowledge of good and evil."

(Genesis 2:7-9, MKJV)

The issue of having to maintain a good and healthy physical diet also had spiritual repercussions. By disrespecting God and eating what was forbidden also indicated that they would pay attention to and happily absorb poisonous spiritual food. If they would listen to the lies of some other being and follow temptation that went against God's clear instructions, they would signal that they were not giving God due honor and respect. It would show a disbelief in their Creator!

> "And Jehovah God took the man and put him into the garden of Eden to work it and keep it. And Jehovah God commanded the man, saying, You may freely eat of every tree in the garden, but you shall not eat of the tree of knowledge of good and evil. For in the day that you eat of it you shall surely die."

(Genesis 2:15-17, MKJV)

A spiritual death would happen the same day that they dishonor God. A distance would develop spiritually. They would not regard, nor retain God's guidance any more, and would drift away. Normal animal life may continue for a while, but spiritual life would end.

God continued with His special creation. Humankind would be given the power of language, something the animals can't do.

> "And out of the ground Jehovah God formed every animal of the field and every fowl of the air, and brought them to Adam to see what he would call them. And whatever Adam called each living creature, that was its name. And Adam gave names to all the cattle, and to the birds of the air, and to every animal of the field. But there was not found a suitable helper for Adam."
> (Genesis 2:19-20, MKJV)

Mankind could form words, and name things. Then he can form sentences, and apply tenses and logic, so that people could discuss not just physical things, but also concepts, and even spiritual things. God could very well discuss instructions, and expect humans to understand, and follow. This was crucial, as humans would form the link between God and the animal kingdom. Humans would receive guidance in how to manage and grow the rest of God's creation, so that paradise could spread worldwide, and happiness and growth could be perpetuated forever.

Furthermore, God would make a woman for a special relationship with the man. This is not like the animals. It was designed by God to be different. It was not going to be even like the apes. A man and women would unite in communion, and be with one another to raise children in God's image, spiritually. This would be a full time job. This way families would form, and communities, and cities, and nations. Man and women would become one physically, mentally, intellectually and spiritually.

"And Jehovah God caused a deep sleep to fall on Adam, and he slept. And He took one of his ribs, and closed up the flesh underneath. And Jehovah God made the rib (which He had taken from the man) into a woman. And He brought her to the man. And Adam said, This is now bone of my bones and flesh of my flesh. She shall be called Woman because she was taken out of man. Therefore shall a man leave his father and his mother, and shall cleave to his wife and they shall be one flesh. And they were both naked, the man and his wife; and they were not ashamed."

(Genesis 2:21-25, MKJV)

God had high hopes for humankind. He had great plans. We all could have lived in utopia. But corruption was near, just around the next tree!

The senior fallen angel was at hand. He had alternative ideas about life. In fact, the knowledge that this humankind could one day be resurrected to eternal life, and become like the Angels was a serious issue. He understood that some of these humans could eventually replace his fallen angels. He had two main goals:

1) Prevent salvation to come to humans. They cannot develop and replace him and his fallen angels.
2) Have them follow his deception and try all kinds of alternative lifestyles, religions, mental outlooks, marriages, existence.

He would start with a simple thing like dietary change. It would show a willingness to disregard God and His instruction.

"Now the serpent was more cunning than any beast of the field which Jehovah God had made. And he said to the woman, Is it so that God has said, You shall not eat of every tree of the garden? And the woman said to the serpent, We may eat of the fruit of the trees of the garden. But of the fruit of the tree which is in the middle of the garden, God has said, You shall not eat of it, neither shall you touch it, lest you die. And the serpent said to the woman, You shall not surely die, for God knows that in the day you eat of it, then your eyes shall be opened, and you shall be as God, knowing good and evil. And when the woman saw that the tree was good for food, and that it was pleasing to the eyes, and a tree to be desired to make wise, she took of its fruit, and ate. She also gave to her husband with her, and he ate."

(Genesis 3:1-6, MKJV)

This was a clear indication as to the way things would be. Mankind would be tempted by Satan and the fallen angels, and would experiment and think up alternate ways. He would eventually learn and understand how wrong those alternate ways would be, and that it would not be pleasing to God at all! Their eyes were now opened to alternate and even evil ways.

"And the eyes of both of them were opened. And they knew that they were naked. And they sewed fig leaves together and made girdles for themselves. And they heard the voice of Jehovah God walking in the garden in the cool of the day. And Adam and his wife hid themselves from the presence of Jehovah God in the middle of the trees of the garden. And Jehovah God called to Adam and said to him, Where are you? And he said, I heard Your voice in the garden, and I was afraid, because I am naked, and I hid myself. And He said, Who told you that you were naked? Have you eaten of the tree which I commanded you that you should not eat? And the man said, The woman whom You gave to be with me, she gave me of the tree, and I ate. And Jehovah God said to the woman, What is this you have done? And the woman said, The serpent deceived me, and I ate. And Jehovah God said to the serpent, Because you have done this you are cursed more than all cattle, and more than every animal of the field. You shall go upon your belly, and you shall eat dust all the days of your life."

(Genesis 3:7-14, MKJV)

The symbolism of the snake indicates the low, devious and sneaky nature of Satan. Here God predicted that one day a man would come that would be totally obedient to God, and overcome Satan and his mentality. This man would bruise the way of thinking of Satan forever, but Satan would be allowed to strike him down temporarily. However, even in striking the man down, Satan will still expose himself to show to humans how evil he is.

That man was Jesus Christ, who came to the woman, the Church Israel gathered in Jerusalem for the festivals.

"And I will put enmity between you and the woman, and between your seed and her Seed; He will bruise your head, and you shall bruise His heel."

(Genesis 3:15, MKJV)

Now God would allow life to become difficult for humans. Because of continual sin, we would suffer unwanted results. Life would be precious, and there would be constant danger to life, due to sin. God did not want it to be, but our sin would bear the pain that we experience.

Humans would need to cover their sins and sinfulness. Even on a spiritual level, we would need a slain animal as a sacrifice to cover our sin, and reduce the shame, and desire for sin. The sacrifice would help to turn us around, away from sin and evil.

"And for Adam and his wife Jehovah God made coats of skins, and clothed them."

(Genesis 3:21, MKJV)

The big problem now was that humans knew from God how to do good, but also tasted freedom to the bad. They listened to Satan, and would have the proclivity to descent into evil ways. That would be destructive to the environment, and humans could not be allowed to destroy God's garden that way. The garden had to stay to be a reminder of how wonderful God's ways would turn out to be. Humans had to keep the longing for utopia, in order to compare with the situation that they developed for themselves due to their sin. Most importantly, humans would have a limited life span, to limit the evil that individuals could cause.

"And Jehovah God said, Behold, the man has become as one of Us, to know good and evil. And now, lest he put forth his hand and take also of the tree of life, and eat, and live forever,

therefore Jehovah God sent him out from the garden of Eden to till the ground from which he had been taken. And He drove out the man. And He placed cherubs at the east of the garden of Eden, and a flaming sword which turned every way, to guard the way to the tree of life."

(Genesis 3:22-24, MKJV)

And so sin entered mankind, and we have to live with it, and see the evil and destruction, and turn to God, seeking Him, and desiring His advice, His Commandments, and ways.

What followed was the constant conflict between good and bad, between God's guidance and human rebellion, between what could have been and what actually happened. We will see this constant theme, of the disobedience and disastrous results.

Humans have the ability to understand and follow God like the Angels, but then somewhere along the line people rebel, and descent into animal ways.

4 History of mankind

We will look at a historic overview of humans reaching to God and growing towards becoming like the good Angels, and others falling back to the animal ways.

In the Old Testament era God reached out to mankind through His good Angels, who often had to resist or confront the bad angels who would try and deceive them and prevent them from fulfilling their assignment. The Angels gave testimony, prophesy and Law through the prophets to the Israelites, who were supposed to hold fast to the Covenant.

> "Which of the prophets did your fathers not persecute?
> And they killed those who foretold the coming of the
> Just One, of whom you have now been the betrayers and
> murderers; who received the Law through disposition of
> angels, and did not keep it."
>
> (Acts 7:52-53, MKJV)

And so there was a continual effort from the Angels on behalf of God. They worked through the prophets to keep Israel in the right spiritual path, but with limited success. We will look at some high and low points.

~~~~~

Cain and Abel

Adam and Eve had limited success with their children. Abel managed to understand true worship of God leading to obedience and a good attitude towards God.
~~~~~

Serving God the way God instructs made Abel happy and blessed, and acceptable to God.

However, Cain did a very halfhearted attempt at serving God. He did not like it, and made things up the way he liked. He in fact reduced the service and made it very easy for himself, being resentful, and having a rebellious attitude towards it.

"And Adam knew Eve his wife. And she conceived and bore Cain, and said, I have gotten a man from Jehovah. And she bore again, his brother Abel. And Abel was a keeper of sheep, but Cain was a tiller of the ground. And in the end of days, it happened, Cain brought to Jehovah an offering of the fruit of the ground. And Abel also brought of the firstlings of his flock and of the fat of it. And Jehovah had respect to Abel and to his offering, but He did not have respect to Cain and to his offering. And Cain glowed with anger, and his face fell. And Jehovah said to Cain, Why have you angrily glowed? And why did your face fall? If you do well, shall you not be accepted? And if you do not do well, sin crouches at the door; and its desire is for you, and you shall rule over it. And Cain talked with his brother Abel. And it happened when they were in the field, Cain rose up against his brother Abel and killed him."

(Genesis 4:1-8, MKJV)

The sloppiness in serving God, doing the wrong things and not according to God's guidance, having a bad attitude and harboring evil thoughts eventually lead to the most horrible sin. While Abel was reaching towards Angel like behavior, Cain descended into pure animal behavior.

"In this the children of God are revealed, and the children of the Devil: everyone not practicing righteousness is not of God, also he who does not love his brother. For this is the message that you have heard from the beginning, that we should love one another;

not as Cain who was of the evil one, and killed his brother. And for what did he kill him? Because his own works were evil, and his brother's things were righteous."

(1 John 3:10-12, MKJV)

Since evil animal-like people tend to hate and even kill Angel-like people, the rest of the story of the first millennium is bad and evil. Only Noah found favor with God, and reach towards becoming an Angel.

"And Jehovah said, My spirit shall not always strive with man, in his erring; he is flesh. Yet his days shall be a hundred and twenty years."

(Genesis 6:3, MKJV)

The Creator now further limits the lifespan of humans, to limit the damage they do, so that younger generations that may turn to God, can have a better chance of survival.

~~~~~

Noah and the Flood

"And Jehovah repented that He had made man on the earth, and He was angry to His heart. And Jehovah said, I will destroy man whom I have created, from the face of the earth, both man, and beast, and the creeping thing,
~~~~~

and the fowls of the air. For I repent that I have made them. But Noah found grace in the eyes of Jehovah."

(Genesis 6:6-8, MKJV)

After a millennium, only Noah reached towards Angel status, and God was going to give the good man and his family a head starts in a new world. They were to be given a free reign to worship God and obey Him, establishing a new society free of fear of other evil people around them. God was going to allow another life extinction event on the earth, which happens regularly. Noah was given prophetic foreknowledge, and could save his family.

Because Noah was righteous and obeyed God, he had faith, and acted on the prophecies. He spent 100 years motivating his family and servants to build the Ark. That faith leading to obedience saved him and his family.

"These are the generations of Noah. Noah was a just man and perfect in his generations. Noah walked with God. And Noah fathered three sons, Shem, Ham, and Japheth. The earth also was corrupt before God, and the earth was filled with violence. And God looked upon the earth. And, behold, it was corrupted! For all flesh had corrupted its way upon the earth. And God said to Noah, The end of all flesh has come before Me, for the earth is filled with violence through them. And, behold, I will destroy them with the earth. Make an ark of cyprus timbers. You shall make rooms in the ark. And you shall pitch it inside and outside with pitch."

(Genesis 6:9-14, MKJV

A new family will be on the earth after all the evil humankind formulating their own ideas of fake gods, fashioning them in their own image in their imaginations, instead of God's image as He orders us, was wiped out. They would have complete religious freedom. Satan's influence was wiped out. Noah and his family would have the perfect start to worship God and reach out to Angel status. But it did not last for long.

Being new to the practice of wine making, Noah misjudged the process, and became intoxicated. One of his the sons did not have much respect for his dad. He certainly did not honor and respect his dad as the others. What his son did was evil again in God's sight. Consider the disrespect, the drift towards animal behavior.

"And Noah began to be a husbandman. And he planted a vineyard. And he drank of the wine and was drunk. And he was uncovered inside his tent. And Ham, the father of Canaan, saw the nakedness of his father, and told his two brothers outside. And Shem and Japheth took a garment and laid it upon both their shoulders. And they went backwards and covered the nakedness of their father. And their faces were backwards, and they did not see their father's nakedness. And Noah awoke from his wine, and came to know what his younger son had done to him. And he said, Cursed be Canaan. He shall be a servant of servants to his brothers."

(Genesis 9:20-25, MKJV)

The reader must understand the language of the Bible as it was written to be very respectful to people. The "nakedness" may have alluded to a much more serious evil desire. To "see the nakedness" of a dad was not just an accidental sighting.

Notice the Law:

"None of you shall approach to any who are near of kin to him, to uncover their nakedness. I am Jehovah."

(Leviticus 18:6, MKJV)

This is not accidental sighting. Later on in the same passage it is made clear:

"And you shall not take a wife to her sister, to vex her, to uncover her nakedness, beside the other in her life. Also you shall not approach to a woman to uncover her nakedness in the impurity of her uncleanness. And you shall not lie carnally with your neighbor's wife, to defile yourself with her."

(Leviticus 18:18-20, MKJV)

It is talking of sex, or at least a desire for sex, or lust. Ham saw his dad drunk, and probably pulled the blanket off to uncover his dad's nakedness, and had evil thoughts at least. We are talking of homosexual ideas! That was totally evil in God's sight, and Noah's sons knew it. Yet Ham did not regard God, nor showed respect to his dad, but instead was contemplating misusing him in his vulnerability, which was totally evil. For that he would be pushed out of the family, and would not inherit land. He would be viewed with suspicion, and constantly be scrutinized for evil tendencies.

~~~~~
~~~~~

Saving Lot from Sodom

Lot decided to live near the city of Sodom, while Abram chose the free countryside. It was more convenient in terms of trade and services, but Sodom had descended into animal behavior. God's good Angels would have to save him.

"And there came two angels to Sodom at evening. And Lot sat in the gate of Sodom. And Lot rose up to meet them when he saw them. And he bowed himself with his face toward the ground, and said, Behold now, my lords, please turn into your servant's house and stay all night, and wash your feet, and you shall rise up early and go your way. And they said, No, but we will stay in the street. But he urgently pressed on them, and they turned in to him and entered into his house. And he made them a feast, and baked unleavened bread, and they ate."

(Genesis 19:1-3, MKJV)

It is clear that Lot didn't like Sodom. He rather stayed at the entrance, so as to not get drawn into the sin happening at night.

"But before they lay down, the men of the city, the men of Sodom, surrounded the house, both old and young, all the people from every quarter. And they called to Lot, and said to him, Where are the men which came in to you this night? Bring them out to us, that we may know them."

(Genesis 19:4-5, MKJV)

In case the reader does not understand what these men of Sodom meant by "knowing" them, it will become very clear. The Bible writers sometimes tried to put things politely. The reality was much, much worse.

> "And Lot went out to the door to them, and shut the door after him. And he said, I pray you, brothers, do not act evilly. Behold now, I have two daughters which have not known man. I pray you, let me bring them out to you, and you do to them as you see fit. But do nothing to these men, for this is why they came under the shadow of my roof."

(Genesis 19:4-5, MKJV)

It must be clear to any honest reader what they were talking about. The women have not known any men before. It obviously talks about sex.

> "And they said, Stand back! And they said, This one came in to stay, and must he judge always? Now we will deal worse with you than with them. And they pressed hard upon the man, Lot, and came near to breaking the door."

(Genesis 19:9, MKJV)

The men of Sodom knew that Lot would judge them for the evil lustful ways. This is a typical reaction of gay people wanting to make sure that straight godly people don't judge them. So these men of Sodom wanted to initiate the visitors to make sure they don't judge the people of Sodom. It was a constant concern of the gay people, hence today they have gay pride parades, where they flaunt their lustful ways before straight and honest godly people.

This is the classical way of making sure gay people are not judged for their filthy ways.

The Angels, which deliberately now appeared as men to test these inhabitants of Sodom, took action to save Lot and his family from the evil and filth of these men!

> "But the men put out their hands and brought Lot into the house to them, and shut the door. And they smote the men that were at the door of the house with blindness, both small and great, so that they wearied themselves to find the door. And the men said to Lot, Have you anyone here besides yourself? Bring your sons-in-law, and your sons, and your daughters, and whatever you have in the city, bring them out of this place. For we will destroy this place because great is the cry of them before the face of Jehovah. And Jehovah has sent us to destroy it."

> (Genesis 10:10-13, MKJV)

The Angels had the power to destroy the gay cities. Fire would come and destroy their homes and towns. This is an ongoing scenario, even today as God allow cities that pander to these gay pride people to burn.

> "And Lot went out and spoke with his sons-in-law, who married his daughters, and said, Get up and get out of this place, for Jehovah will destroy this city. But he seemed as one that mocked to his sons-in-law."

> (Genesis 19:14, MKJV)

These sons-in-law did not understand the true Faith. They did not believe in the power of these Angels. So they tarried, and died as well!

"And when the dawn rose up, then the angels hurried Lot, saying, Rise up! Take your wife and your two daughters who are here, lest you be consumed in the iniquity of the city. And he lingered, the angel laid hold upon his hand, and upon the hand of his wife, and upon the hand of his two daughters (Jehovah being merciful to him), and they brought him forth and set him outside the city."

(Genesis 19:15-16, MKJV)

And the result was that the gay pride people of Sodom and Gomorrah were destroyed. God is not mocked. Animal behavior will be destroyed among humans. And when they vexed and threatened Lot who was reaching out to God and His righteous Angels and correct behavior, God would not let that carry on. Cities and neighborhoods like these are in grave danger.

"Then Jehovah rained upon Sodom and upon Gomorrah brimstone and fire, from Jehovah out of the heavens."

(Genesis 19:24, MKJV)

Later these daughters committed a further crime, having been tainted by the promiscuity of Sodom, and their offspring became enemies of Israel, and for hundreds of years was a thorn in Israel's side. Israel had to make war and kill many of them over the years to ensure its existence and safety. God and His Angels will never condone this kind of animal behavior!

Abraham, Isaac and Jacob

Abraham believed and obeyed God, and taught his children to worship God. He taught them to keep the Commandments, and follow God's instructions. Because of obedience, God had high hopes for his family, and decided to bless them with their own country in which they would implement God's Law.

"And I will make your seed to multiply as the stars of the heavens, and will give to your seed all these lands. And in your Seed shall all the nations of the earth be blessed, because Abraham obeyed My voice and kept My charge, My commandments, My statutes, and My Laws."

(Genesis 26:4-5, MKJV)

For this reason, the Angels were involved, and God ordered them to protect the family, and intervene when necessary. Through the family of Abraham, a whole generation and later a whole nation had the opportunity to reach towards Angel status.

And so Isaac was next in line, and also taught his son Jacob. The inheritance of Israel belongs to them, and they reached out to Angel status, repenting from sin, and stayed faithful. The Angels certainly took notice, and gave Jacob a vision of his incredible potential, and future existence.

"And he dreamed. And behold! A ladder was set up on the earth, and the top of it reached to Heaven! And behold! The angels of God were ascending and descending on it! And behold! Jehovah stood above it, and said, I am Jehovah, the God of Abraham your father, and the God of Isaac! The land on which you lie I will give to you and to your seed. And your seed shall be like the dust of the earth, and you shall spread abroad to the west, and to the east, and to the north, and to the south. And in you and in your Seed shall all the families of the earth be blessed. And, behold, I am with you, and will keep you in every place where you go, and will bring you again into this land. For I will not leave you until I have done that which I have spoken of to you. And Jacob awakened from his sleep. And he said, Surely Jehovah is in this place, and I did not know. And he was afraid, and said, How fearful is this place! This is nothing but the house of God, and this is the gate of Heaven!"

(Genesis 28:12-17, MKJV)

Few men reached this kind of rapport with the Angels of God. Israel drifted away because children were perhaps not taught, and people became too materialistic, and spent too much time making money instead of fulfilling their real mission in life – reaching out to Angel status. But more will achieve this, after the coming of Messiah.

5 Closer to God

Jesus Christ was with God from the beginning, even before the physical creation. The Father created Angels through Christ, and later created the universe through Christ and the Angels. With Jesus as the Son of God walking the earth about two thousand years ago, mankind at that time came closer to God, and we were also given a lot more insights into the relationship with God and His Angels, through the leadership and sacrificial life of Jesus Christ.

When Jesus walked the earth, the Devil came to tempt Him. Jesus was quite strong enough and wise enough to resist the Devil and his evil and deceptive ways.

"Then the Devil took Him up into the holy city and set Him upon a pinnacle of the Temple. And he said to Him, If you are the Son of God, cast yourself down. For it is written, "He shall give His angels charge concerning You, and in their hands they shall bear You up, lest at any time You dash Your foot against a stone." Jesus said to him, It is written again, "You shall not tempt the Lord your God."

(Matthew 4:5-7, MKJV)

Jesus showed that we should not deliberately enter into a contest for self-glory and try and force protection from God and His Angels, but should stand and confront the Devil and his fallen angels. We should not waste the Angels' time with petty demands. Don't fool around.

Jesus and His Ministry extend to us today, and the true teachers and evangelists teach the worship of God, and the keeping of His Commandments. The true worshipper learn from God, follow His instructions, and are led by Jesus through the Word of God, aided by the Spirit that motivates us. The Angels take notice and protects and guides us, till the return of Christ, or our natural death after which come our resurrection to eternal life.

"He answered and said to them, He who sows the good seed is the Son of Man; the field is the world; the good seed are the sons of the kingdom; but the darnel are the sons of the evil one. The enemy who sowed them is the Devil; the harvest is the end of the world; and the reapers are the angels."

(Matthew 13:37-39, MKJV)

Many Christians will reach Angel status. The Angels will know us and be glad to see us resurrected to join them in worshipping God and furthering His goals in expanding and managing His creation for all eternity.

"For the Son of Man shall come in the glory of His Father with His angels, and then He shall reward each one according to his works. Truly I say to you, There are some standing here who shall not taste of death until they see the Son of Man coming in His kingdom."

(Matthew 16:27-28, MKJV)

Then a few days later Jesus showed them how it will be at the return of Messiah.

"And after six days Jesus took Peter, James, and John his brother, and brought them up into a high mountain apart. And He was transfigured before them. And His face shone as the sun, and His clothing was white as the light. And behold, there appeared to them Moses and Elijah talking with Him."

(Matthew 17:1-3, MKJV)

This was the vision Jesus promised that they would see. They saw the return of Jesus at the end of the age, and Moses and Elijah resurrected. They already achieved Angel status! This is what God offers those who obey Him.

"For in the resurrection they neither marry nor are given in marriage, but are as the angels of God in Heaven."

(Matthew 22:30, MKJV)

The reproductive process happens in the physical life of humans on the earth today. Those who turn to God to keep His Commandments and learn to love God and His ways of life and being can be resurrected to eternal life and be like the Angels.

The earth is the training ground. Here we suffer pain and death for transgressions and being like animals instead of becoming like Angels worshipping God. Once we are selected and resurrected to eternal life, we are among Angels and will have the opportunity to beautify and restore earth to the way God wanted initially. This will happen in the millennial rule of Christ.

In the Old Covenant people had to sacrifice lambs to try and come to terms with their destructive ways, but it was not completely effective. After Christ's sacrifice we realize that our destructive ways killed the Son of God. Judgment is given to Jesus to decide who will be resurrected to eternal life at His return. We realize that continual transgression of God's Commandments is destructive and would ruin paradise. We see the result of mankind's attitudes in the crucifixion of the same Jesus Christ, the Son of God, the very One who came to help us, to save us from our sins. This is far more effective, and leads to permanent repentance. This makes it possible to reach Angel status.

The current trend of mankind in all its sinful ways is towards global destruction, which God will allow, but not complete life extinction. Those left from all the wars, pollution and pandemics will seek a savior to stop the madness. Jesus will be sent to turn things around.

"And immediately after the tribulation of those days, the sun shall be darkened and the moon shall not give her light, and the stars shall fall from the heaven, and the powers of the heavens shall be shaken. And then the sign of the Son of Man shall appear in the heavens. And then all the tribes of the earth shall mourn, and they shall see the Son of Man coming in the clouds of the heaven with power and great glory. And He shall send His angels with a great sound of a trumpet, and they shall gather His elect from the four winds, from one end of the heavens to the other."

(Matthew 24:29-31, MKJV)

The people of WWIII, when economic collapse happens, and various pandemics sweep through the world, And pollution will make the earth no longer able to sustain life, and starvation and death and burials is a daily routine, will seek for a Messiah, and will morn at His return, understanding that they vilified Him, and believed in a creation without a creator, and became like animals. Rulers of the world with their corrupt industry leaders will know their corruption will finally be fully exposed, and judgment is at hand. All people will morn. But Jesus will turn things around for the good of all mankind.

> "Truly I say to you, This generation shall not pass until all these things are fulfilled. The heaven and the earth shall pass away, but My Words shall not pass away. But of that day and hour no one knows, no, not the angels of Heaven, but only My Father. But as the days of Noah were, so shall be the coming of the Son of Man."

(Matthew 24:34-37, MKJV)

Jesus will take drastic measures to turn things on the earth around, and prepare for His millennial rule. The Angels will help Him, and also those good and faithful Christians resurrected to become like the Angels. They would bring the experience of the pain of animal life, together with having worked to become more Angel like to bear on the process of bringing more people to salvation in the seventh millennium. Hence as new Angels they would know how to rule to turn the world around towards utopia.

> "But when the Son of Man comes in His glory, and all the holy angels with Him, then He shall sit on the throne of His glory. And all nations shall be gathered before Him. And He shall separate them from one another, as a shepherd divides the sheep from the goats. And indeed He shall set the sheep on His right hand, but the goats off the left. Then the King shall say to those on His right hand, Come, blessed of My Father, inherit the kingdom prepared for you from the foundation of the world."

(Matthew 25:31-34, MKJV)

The world will eventually all turn to God and His Son. The earth will be cleaned up. Corruption will be rooted out. Sin will be abolished. Paradise will grow, thanks to those who became like the Angels. They will know how bad it can be for physical animals, having grown up as an animal, somewhat like an ape, but have studied God Word, the Bible, and having reach out to God, to follow His Son, and become more and more like Angels. They will even be given power over the fallen angels.

"Do you not know that we shall judge angels, not to mention the things of this life?"

(1 Corinthians 6:3, MKJV)

The quest for Angel status is something that anybody can aspire to. We are initially like apes. But we were created to have special capabilities, to communicate, read and write, to understand concepts of God. It is possible to follow Jesus Christ to become like the Angels. The path is open to us!

"But one testified in a certain place, saying, "What is man, that You are mindful of him; or the son of man, that You visit him? You have made him a little lower than the angels. You crowned him with glory and honor and set him over the works of Your hands. You subjected all things under his feet." For in subjecting all things to Him, He did not leave anything not subjected to Him. But now we do not see all things having been subjected to him. But we see Jesus, who was made a little lower than the angels for the suffering of death, crowned with glory and honor, that He by the grace of God should taste death for all. For it became Him, for whom are all things and by whom are all things, in bringing many sons into glory, to perfect the Captain of their salvation through sufferings."

(Hebrews 2:6-10, MKJV)

Jesus was made perfect through His sufferings. His followers will also be made perfect through their sufferings, returning good for the evil that the world brings on its citizens. This way they become more like Angels, and a record is written in Heaven about their goodness.

"Behold, I give to you authority to tread on serpents and scorpions, and over all the authority of the enemy. And nothing shall by any means hurt you. Yet do not rejoice in this, that the evil spirits are subject to you, rather rejoice because your names are written in Heaven."

(Luke 10:19-20, MKJV)

In Jesus we can see the spiritual reality of what was portrayed in the physical reality of the rituals of the Old Testament. Those who still insist on that ritual and reject Christ as having fulfilled the ritual, and rejecting His supreme sacrificial life, are putting a veil over their own spiritual eyes, refusing to see how Jesus showed the way to eternal life with the Angels.

"But we all, with our face having been unveiled, having beheld the glory of the Lord as in a mirror, are being changed into the same image from glory to glory, even as by the Lord Spirit."

(2 Corinthians 3:18, MKJV)

The Angels beheld how the Master of our salvation let go of His glory with the Father, and was born a human being, to have become subject to death, and yet still maintained His righteousness and unwavering faith and obedience in the face of our sinfulness.

In the book to the Hebrews the situation is well explained:

"being made so much better than the angels, as He has by inheritance obtained a more excellent name than they. For to which of the angels did He say at any time, "You are My Son, this day I have begotten You?" And again, "I will be to Him a Father, and He shall be to Me a Son?" And again, when He brings in the First-born into the world, He says, "And let all the angels of God worship Him." And of the angels He says, "Who makes His angels spirits and His ministers a flame of fire." But to the Son He says, "Your throne, O God, is forever and ever. A scepter of righteousness is the scepter of Your kingdom. You have loved righteousness and hated iniquity, therefore God, Your God, has anointed You with the oil of gladness above Your fellows." "You, Lord, have laid the foundation of the earth in the beginning, and the heavens are the works of Your hands. They shall perish, but You will remain. And they shall all become old as a garment, and as a covering You shall fold them up, and they shall be changed. But You are the same, and Your years shall not fail." But to which of the angels, did He say at any time, "Sit on My right hand until I make Your enemies Your footstool?" Are they not all ministering spirits, sent forth to minister for those who shall be heirs of salvation?"

(Hebrews 1:4-14, MKJV)

The true saints will be given the opportunity in the resurrection to rule with Christ, having been in the flesh and yet having overcome the downward spiral to ape behavior, to become more like Jesus Christ, having worked at their salvation, following Jesus Christ, ceased from sin, from the transgressions against the Commandments of the New Covenant. They will know how to succeed against all odds, to rule over the temptations of the fallen angels, wanting them to descend into wild animal behavior. Those who overcome will be given the coming Kingdom of Jesus Christ which will be manifested in the seventh millennium.

"For He has not put in subjection to the angels the world to come, of which we speak. But one testified in a certain place, saying, "What is man, that You are mindful of him; or the son of man, that You visit him? You have made him a little lower than the angels. You crowned him with glory and honor and set him over the works of Your hands. You subjected all things under his feet." For in subjecting all things to Him, He did not leave anything not subjected to Him. But now we do not see all things having been subjected to him. But we see Jesus, who was made a little lower than the angels for the suffering of death, crowned with glory and honor, that He by the grace of God should taste death for all. For it became Him, for whom are all things and by whom are all things, in bringing many sons into glory, to perfect the Captain of their salvation through sufferings. For both He who sanctifies and they who are sanctified are all of One, for which cause He is not ashamed to call them brothers, saying, "I will declare Your name to My brothers; in the midst of the assembly I will sing praise to You." And again, "I will put My trust in Him." And again, "Behold Me and the children whom God has given Me." Since then the children have partaken of flesh and blood, He also Himself likewise partook of the same; that through death He might destroy him who had the power of death (that is, the Devil), and deliver those who through fear of death were all their lifetime subject to bondage. For truly He did not take the nature of angels, but He took hold of the seed of Abraham. Therefore in all things it behoved him to be made like His brothers, that He might be a merciful and faithful high priest in things pertaining to God, to make propitiation for the sins of His people. For in that He Himself has suffered, having been tempted, He is able to rescue those who are being tempted."

(Hebrews 2:5-18, MKJV)

Jesus is now also the ruler over the Angels, as He is the ruler over Christians.

"who is at the right hand of God, having gone into Heaven, where the angels and authorities and powers are being subjected to Him."

(1 Peter 3:22, MKJV)

The fallen angels are kept and bound from doing more damage to the Creation. Before humans existed on the earth, these fallen angels were created and charged with managing affair on the earth. But we see that some corrupted their ways, being swayed by Satan, and face eternal expulsion by Jesus Christ.

"And those angels not having kept their first place, but having deserted their dwelling-place, He has kept in everlasting chains under darkness for the judgment of a great Day;"

(Jude 1:6, MKJV)

A summary of what would happen in the past two millenniums was revealed to Christians. The successful struggle against evil fallen angels, and in particular Satan, was portrayed. Jesus Christ would lead in this struggle, with the righteous Angels to succeed. Saints would also be perfected, and overcome, to reign with Christ and the righteous Angels in the seventh millennial rule of Christ, to turn this world around, and make it the utopia God envisioned from the beginning. Satan and his fallen angels will not have wanted this to be so.

It was ordained that Jesus would be born in Israel, near Jerusalem, while the sons of Abraham lived there, and had some rule on the spiritual level. Israel was seen as the woman that would give birth to Jesus, a Jew, according to the promises made to Abraham, the father of the twelve tribes. It was a stressful time for Israel, with the Roman occupation, and the threat of shutting down the Temple services.

"And there appeared a great sign in the heavens, a woman clothed with the sun, and the moon was under her feet, and a crown of twelve stars on her head, and having a babe in womb, she cries, being in travail, having been distressed to bear."

(Revelation 12:1-2, MKJV)

The Devil and his fallen angels did not want to have this happen. Jesus would succeed in obedience to God and His

Commandments in humility, where Satan became bashful and selfish, and wanted to rule as he saw fit.

"And another sign was seen in the heavens. And behold a great red dragon, having seven heads and ten horns and seven crowns on his heads! And his tail drew the third part of the stars of heaven, and cast them onto the earth. And the dragon stood before the woman being about to bear, so that when she bears he might devour her child."

(Revelation 12:3-4, MKJV)

Jesus was given space to fulfill His ministry, being protected by God and the righteous Angels.

"And she bore a son, a male, who is going to rule all nations with a rod of iron. And her child was caught up to God and to His throne."

(Revelation 12:5, MKJV)

After the fulfillment of the promises to Abraham in the ministry of Jesus Christ, and the expanded fulfillment of the Sign of Jonah giving Jerusalem forty years to repent, the wrath of the Roman Empire came to bear on the Temple, where military rulers apparently demanded to have a pig sacrificed on the Altar, which was of course refused, leading to the destruction of the Temple, as Jesus foretold.

"And the woman fled into the wilderness, where she had a place prepared by God, so that they might nourish her there a thousand, two hundred and sixty days."

(Revelation 12:6, MKJV)

The Church fathers were warned to flee to the mountains, which they did, and survived between the rocks of Petra. They were nourished by the ruler of Petra, who gave them favor, while some Jews also held out on the mount at Masada.

Satan was obviously furious, and demanded space to persecute the Church in the wilderness. But the Church kept the Faith, and would not compromise the Truth.

"And there was war in Heaven. Michael and his angels warring against the dragon. And the dragon and his angels warred, but did not prevail. Nor was place found for them in Heaven any more. And the great dragon was cast out, the old serpent called Devil, and Satan, who deceives the whole world. He was cast out into the earth, and his angels were cast out with him. And I heard a great voice saying in Heaven, Now has come the salvation and power and the kingdom of our God, and the authority of His Christ. For the accuser of our brothers is cast down, who accused them before our God day and night. And they overcame him because of the blood of the Lamb, and because of the word of their testimony. And they did not love their soul until death."

(Revelation 12:7-11, MKJV)

Satan now knew that his reign over the nations of the earth, and opportunity to continue with the greedy confrontational ways causing wars, would come to an end one day. Saints prevail in the way of obedience to God, and making peace among humans.

"Therefore rejoice, O heavens, and those tabernacling in them. Woe to the inhabitants of the earth and in the sea!

For the Devil came down to you, having great wrath, knowing that he has but a little time. And when the dragon saw that he was cast to the earth, he persecuted the woman who bore the man child ."

(Revelation 12:12-13, MKJV)

So Jerusalem was destroyed, and Jews scattered into the Roman Empire. The Church would also be scattered after Masada was conquered, and soldiers also reached Petra. But the Apostles would continue in their ministries preaching everywhere they came, as far as Scotland, India and Ethiopia. The armies pursued, but drought in places and frost in others, and other calamities made them stop their quest to root out Christianity.

"And two wings of a great eagle were given to the woman, so that she might fly into the wilderness, into her place, where she is nourished for a time and times and half a time, from the serpent's face. And the serpent cast out of his mouth water like a flood after the woman, so that he might cause her to be carried away by the river. And the earth helped the woman. And the earth opened its mouth and swallowed up the river which the dragon cast out of his mouth. And the dragon was enraged over the woman, and went to make war with the rest of her seed, who keep the commandments of God and have the testimony of Jesus Christ."

(Revelation 12:14-17, MKJV)

The confrontation between the fallen angels and the righteous Angels would continue to play out on the earth because it is mankind's choice to ignore the God of the Bible. Like Adam and Eve, we still want to do our own thing, formulate our own ideas of how we apparently evolved from one of the ape species, while we can't explain why none of the other ape species evolved as well. Humans prefer to believe the scientists are true, making assumptions about all the gaps in their theories, while not seriously proving whether the Bible is true. As long as mankind don't reach out to God and His Son, Jesus the Christ, the fallen angels will still carry on trying their ideas on all kinds of different governance models. Corruption will continue. Pollution will continue. And prophecies of wars will be fulfilled.

"Jesus said to him, You shall love the Lord your God with all your heart, and with all your soul, and with all your mind. This is the first and great commandment. And the second is like it, You shall love your neighbor as yourself. On these two commandments hang all the Law and the Prophets."

(Matthew 22:37-40, MKJV)

The prophecies of the prophets will continue as long as the world does not follow these two Commandments, and the first and second great commandments are explained in the first five and second five commandments.

But fortunately, there will always be saints around the world that study and prove, and keep the Ten Commandments of God, and are allowed to further the true testimony of Jesus Christ.

" … who keep the commandments of God and have the testimony of Jesus Christ."

(Revelation 12:14-17, MKJV)

And as the true Gospel spreads, and saints learn to love the Commandments of God, and teach about Jesus the Christ, and His sacrificial life, and repent to love His ways of truth, honesty, fairness all based on the Ten Commandments of God, there will always be a chance for people to reach Angel status.

Thanks to Jesus the Christ, many people will get closer to God. Many will convert and believe the Bible, after long and hard study, proving the Word of God to be true. Many will repent and keep the Commandments of God. Many will become saints, and will reach Angel status. The sum of saints needed to join Jesus Christ to begin the seventh millennial rule of Christ will be filled.

The saints don't have to physically fight for Jesus. The fight is spiritual, for truth, knowledge and to be free from sin. But the righteous Angels in Heaven will fight Satan and his fallen angels, and bring them down one day, to allow Jesus Christ to return and take over Jerusalem, and Israel, and also eventually the whole world and all its kingdoms, so that true liberty can break free, free from corruption, free from crime, free from hunger, sin and war.

The seventh millennium is coming near. Humans will eventually experience utopia!

6 The seventh millennium

Some other religions believe their followers must take up arms and fight for their beliefs and leadership, even dead leadership. True Christianity does not have to do that. God's Angels will bring on the promised seventh millennium, that will see Jesus Christ return from Heaven, and will begin the process of bring peace to the world, and a utopian society for all.

The saints on the earth cannot bring it on. It is not possible. It is not expected. The saints are peaceful loving people. However, when God brings it on, nothing can stop it.

Mankind in general will not have enough Biblical knowledge to understand when it happens. So unfortunately mankind in general will initially resist the coming of Messiah. The biggest loser will be Satan and his fallen angels. For mankind in the long term it will be a great turn of events. Into the seventh millennium, people will look back at the traumatic times that they went through, and understand that humans brought it on themselves.

We only have one planet on which to survive. God has ordained that we will face the consequences of polluting our only home. Humans must understand and feel the damage done to life on the earth. That's why we are half ape like. We will suffer with the animals, so that those who became like the Angels will love the animals with compassion.

Large corporations are ruthlessly polluting the earth, and it will come back to haunt us. Governments are turning a blind eye to all the corruption that is robbing citizens from a decent life. More is spent on armaments than on helping the poor. And it has to stop.

A vision of what will happen in Heaven at the time is portrayed in Revelation 19. The vision is symbolic in many ways. For instance, the sword coming out of Christ's mouth is not physical. It is His spoken word, cutting through the deception and lies of false preachers, and religious authorities, and governments using them. The slaying with that sword is obviously not literally with blood spattering everywhere. It is the slaying of people even in universities that teach their assumptions, causing students to believe their theories as real. It is kings and presidents resigning because people have realized that they were lied to. It is college professors resigning because they put forth theory as fact. It is false preachers who lied and resigned because people would know they were deceived.

Let's look at what will happen in Heaven at that time:

"And after these things I heard a great sound of a numerous crowd in Heaven, saying, Hallelujah! Salvation and glory and honor and the power to the Lord our God! For true and righteous are His judgments. For He has judged the great harlot who defiled the earth with her fornication, and He has avenged the blood of His servants out of her hand. And secondly they said, Hallelujah! And her smoke rose up forever and ever. And the twenty-four elders and the four living creatures fell down and worshiped God sitting on the throne, saying, Amen! Hallelujah! And a voice came out of the throne, saying, Praise our God, all His servants, and the ones fearing Him, the small and great. And I heard as the sound of a great multitude, and as the sound of many waters, and as the sound of strong thunders, saying, Hallelujah! For the Lord God omnipotent reigns!"

(Revelation 19:1-6, MKJV)

God allows Satan and his fallen angels to reign on earth because it was the choice of Adam and Eve, and almost all of their children, and even today.

But some turns to Messiah, believe the Gospel of the coming Kingdom of God, repent from breaking the Commandments of God, and turn to a righteous life, becoming more like the righteous Angels. They will be resurrected at Christ's return.

"Let us be glad and rejoice and we will give glory to Him. For the marriage of the Lamb has come, and His wife has prepared herself. And to her was granted that she should be arrayed in fine linen, clean and white. For the fine linen is the righteousness of the saints. And he said to me, Write, Blessed are those who have been called to the marriage supper of the Lamb. And he said to me, These are the true sayings of God. And I fell at his feet to worship him. And he said to me, See, do not do it! I am your fellow servant, and of your brothers who have the testimony of Jesus. Worship God, for the testimony of Jesus is the spirit of prophecy."

(Revelation 19:7-10, MKJV)

The righteous Angels are fellow servants just as the saints and evangelists are on the earth. We work together for the good of mankind.

The white horse in the following section is a vision of what will happen spiritually, when Jesus Christ will return to preach powerfully and personally to all the earth. He will lead by fair and just Law, like a scroll in a golden pipe in a parliament setting, and that Law of God will be enforced in all fairness and justice.

"And I saw Heaven opened. And behold, a white horse! And He sitting on him was called Faithful and True. And in righteousness He judges and makes war. And His eyes were like a flame of fire, and on His head many crowns. And He had a name written, one that no one knew except Himself. And He had been clothed in a garment dipped in blood, and His name is called The Word of God. And the armies in Heaven followed Him on white horses, clothed in fine linen, white and clean. And out of His mouth goes a sharp sword, so that with it He should strike the nations. And He will shepherd them with a rod of iron. And He treads the winepress of the wine of the anger and of the wrath of Almighty God. And He has on His garment, and on His thigh a name written, KING OF KINGS AND LORD OF LORDS. And I saw one angel standing in the sun. And he cried with a great voice, saying to all the birds that fly in mid-heaven, Come and gather together to the supper of the great God, so that you may eat the flesh of kings, and the flesh of commanders, and the flesh of strong ones, and the flesh of horses, and those sitting on them, and the flesh of all, both free and slave, both small and great."

(Revelation 19:11-18, MKJV)

But the world and its misguided leaders and all false religious leaders will still deceive most of the world to resist the coming of Messiah and the Kingdom of God.

"And I saw the beast, and the kings of the earth and their armies, being gathered to make war against Him who sat on the horse, and against His army. And the beast was taken, and with him the false prophet doing signs before it, (by which he deceived those who had received the mark of the beast), and those who had worshiped his image. The two were thrown alive into the Lake of Fire burning with brimstone. And the rest were slain by the sword of Him who sat on the horse, it proceeding out of His mouth. And all the birds were filled from their flesh."

(Revelation 19:19-21, MKJV)

Al the wrong teachings and deception will be eradicated and truth about God and Messiah will spread like a wildfire. Satan will lose his position of power and will no longer influence events on the earth, causing wars.

"And I saw an angel come down from Heaven, having the key of the abyss and a great chain in his hand. And he laid hold on the dragon, that old serpent, who is the Devil and Satan, and bound him a thousand years. And he cast him into the abyss and shut him up and set a seal on him, that he should deceive the nations no more until the thousand years should be fulfilled. And after that he must be loosed a little time."

(Revelation 20:1-3, MKJV)

The thousand year millennial reign of Messiah will finally happen. The saints will be resurrected and together with the righteous Angels will be given the chance to rule the earth spiritually. There will only be one religion on the earth, only one Church.

"And I saw thrones, and they sat on them, and judgment was given to them. And I saw the souls of those who had been beheaded for the witness of Jesus and for the Word of God, and who had not worshiped the beast nor his image, nor had received his mark on their foreheads, nor in their hands. And they lived and reigned with Christ a thousand years."

(Revelation 20:4, MKJV)

The Bible shows two resurrections. The first happens at the return of Messiah. The saints will have the opportunity to reign spiritually with the righteous Angels, for they would have overcome sin, and also have experience with physical life to understand how important it is to care for the animals. The vision of God is clear:

"They will not labor in vain, nor bring forth for terror. For they are the seed of the beloved of Jehovah, and their offspring with them. And it will be, before they call I will answer; and while they are still speaking, I will hear. The wolf and the lamb will feed together, and the lion will eat straw like the ox; and dust will be the food of the snake. They will not hurt nor destroy in all My holy mountain, says Jehovah."

(Isaiah 65:23-25, MKJV)

Let's continue with the vision of the millennial reign of Messiah:

The second resurrection will be for all people who have not repented perhaps due to misguided teachings, misguided religions, and misguided education. There are also those who have not even read the Word of God. There are billions who can't even own a Bible.

Today the saints look into the Law of liberty, God's Ten Commandments, and allow it to judge them, repenting today of their sins. Others will be judged in the second resurrection, being judged by the same Law of Liberty, and they will all learn to love the Commandments and be saved becoming like the righteous Angels, but some will still refuse, and be left to die in yet another life extinction event.

"But the rest of the dead did not live again until the thousand years were finished. This is the first resurrection. Blessed and holy is he who has part in the first resurrection. The second death has no authority over these, but they will be priests of God and of Christ, and will reign with Him a thousand years. And when the thousand years have expired, Satan will be loosed out of his prison. And he will go out to deceive the nations which are in the four quarters of the earth, Gog and Magog, to gather them together to battle. The number of them is as the sand of the sea. And they went up over the breadth of the earth and circled around the camp of the saints, and the beloved city. And fire came down from God out of Heaven and devoured them. And the Devil who deceived them was cast into the Lake of Fire and Brimstone, where the beast and the false prophet were . And he will be tormented day and night forever and ever. And I saw a great white throne, and Him sitting on it, from whose face the earth and the heaven fled away. And a place was not found for them. And I saw the dead, the small and the great, stand before God. And books were opened, and another book was opened, which is the Book of Life. And the dead were judged out of those things which were written in the books, according to their works. And the sea gave up the dead in it. And death and hell delivered up the dead in them. And each one of them was judged according to their works. And death and hell were cast into the Lake of Fire. This is the second death. And if anyone was not found having been written in the Book of Life, he was cast into the Lake of Fire."

(Revelation 20:5-15, MKJV)

And so our labor of love in Jesus Christ will never be in vain. The good life of Christians will not be in vain, but will still be rewarded. Jesus Christ did not die in vain on the crucifix, but will reign over all the earth eventually.

It is a good story for all humanity. Most of the physically created humans will ultimately grow into Angels that live forever!

7 Beware the fallen angels

Many times some who want to pretend to be holy have alleged that they have seen an angel. Some have claimed that they have communicated with an angel, and received a message. A few have even alleged that an angel have given them information to write a book, which should be added to the Bible.

Can that be true? How do we know for sure?

We know that there are fallen angels. Some have turned away from God, and were separated from the righteous Angels. We have to be able to know which is which. Fortunately there are guidelines given to us thousands of years ago. Many, who have ignored those, have fallen for false leaders and prophets to their own damage.

Jesus Christ in the Flesh

Here is the first indication given:

"And He called the Twelve and began to send them out by two and two. And He gave them authority over unclean spirits,"

(Mark 6:7, MKJV)

Be aware that the twelve apostles appointed over the twelve tribes of Israel would know the difference. Let's see what they wrote to us in this day and age.

"Beloved, do not believe every spirit, but try the spirits to see if they are of God, because many false prophets have gone out into the world."

(1 John 4:1, MKJV)

So don't just fall for any person that alleges that he or she had contact with an angel. It could be a trap. It could be an unclean spirit, a fallen angel. These fallen angels are not red in color with little horns! They may appear to be good angels.

"For such ones are false apostles, deceitful workers, transforming themselves into the apostles of Christ. Did not even Satan marvelously transform himself into an angel of light?"

(2 Corinthians 11:13-14, MKJV)

So here is the first test, given by one of those 12 Apostles that were given power and insight over the fallen angels:

"By this you know the Spirit of God: every spirit that confesses that Jesus Christ has come in the flesh is of God; and every spirit that does not confess that Jesus Christ has come in the flesh is not of God. And this is the antichrist you heard is coming, and even now is already in the world."

(1 John 4:2-3, MKJV)

Any spirit or angel that denies that Jesus is the Christ, the Son of God, and was truly and fully in the flesh as a human being, is not from God, and is a fallen angel. This antichrist teaching was already going forth towards the end of the first century. It has spread worldwide today. This is a serious consideration.

There are people and organizations that talks of Jesus, but will they declare that Jesus is the Christ, the Messiah prophesied to come two thousand years ago, and also prophesied to return to assume total guidance and rule over all the earth? And will they accept that Jesus fully came in the flesh, subject to death?

> "But we see Jesus, who was made a little lower than the angels for the suffering of death, crowned with glory and honor, that He by the grace of God should taste death for all."

(Hebrews 2:9, MKJV)

This is a crucial element of the Faith, and a test of the spirits.

~~~~~

The Two Witnesses

In serious matters, where the path of humanity and the road to salvation was at stake, be aware that God always provide two witnesses. The serious student of the scriptures will be aware of that:
~~~~~

1) Ezra and Nehemiah, together with Daniel causing the rebuilding of the Temple of God.
2) Isaiah and Jeremiah, dealing with the wayward kings of Israel.
3) John the Baptist and Jesus the Christ, heralding the New Covenant, beginning the New Testament era.
4) The Two Witnesses, in the final Last Days just before the return of Jesus the Christ.

Any person coming with an alleged new chapter or book to be added to the Bible and making big changes will have been prophesied about in detail, and there will be two, who often seem to come from different locations, but yet give the very same message.

~~~~~

Keep the Commandments

The Commandments of God was thundered by the voice of God over his people, Israel, during the Exodus.

The same Commandments of the Old Testament is still the Commandments that we subscribe to in the New Covent. The way it is enacted and established and maintained is new, as we have a new Lamb, a new High Priest.

So beware any prophet that claims to have seen an angel, and comes with new material, and different Commandments.

"you shall not listen to the words of that prophet or that dreamer of dreams. For Jehovah your God is testing you to know whether you love Jehovah your God with all your heart and with all your soul. You shall walk after
~~~~~

Jehovah your God and fear Him, and **keep His commandments**, and obey His voice, and you shall serve Him and hold fast to Him."

(Deuteronomy 13:3-4, MKJV)

Any prophet that suggests new commandments should be ignored. The Ten Commandments always stand even into the seventh millennium after Christ's return, and that includes the seventh day Sabbath.

~~~~~

Salvation is complete

The path to eternal life has been opened by Jesus the Christ, through His supreme sacrificial life, and being the final Lamb of God. He did it all according to the prophecies of the Old Testament era. It was actually nothing radically new. Gospel writes goes to great length to highlight how Jesus fulfilled one prophecy after another, even on time as prophesied. That made Him the Messiah, the greatest Prophet. The warning from the original scriptures is that we must ignore a prophet or anybody that alleged that they met an angel or being involved with any spirit that comes with something radically new.

"Do not think that I have come to destroy the Law or the Prophets. I have not come to destroy but to fulfill. For truly I say to you, Till the heaven and the earth pass away, not one jot or one tittle shall in any way pass from the Law until all is fulfilled."

(Matthew 5:17-18, MKJV)
~~~~~

This same Jesus the Christ, the greatest Prophet, secured the only path to salvation. And He gave the final piece of prophecy to mankind. Notice the first few words in Revelation, the last book in the Bible:

"A Revelation of Jesus Christ, which God gave to Him to declare to His servants things which must shortly come to pass. And He signified it by sending His angel to His servant John,"

(Revelation 1:1, MKJV)

The book of Revelation shows all prophecies until the return of Jesus the Christ, the Son of God. And there will be no more.

"For I testify together to everyone who hears the Words of the prophecy of this Book: If anyone adds to these things, God will add on him the plagues that have been written in this Book. And if anyone takes away from the Words of the Book of this prophecy, God will take away his part out of the Book of Life, and out of the holy city, and from the things which have been written in this Book."

(Revelation 22:18-19, MKJV)

Anybody that comes with another book or prophecy that tries to have it added to the Bible as a requirement for salvation will suffer the consequences of the words of Revelation till they stop or be stopped by the coming Messiah: droughts and economic failures, disease epidemics, wars and rumors of wars.

The path to salvation is complete. All Commandments and laws are in the Bible. All prophecies have been given. There is no further information. Mankind have not search and studied even half of what is needed. The books are complete. The Bible is complete.

The way to become like the righteous Angels is in the Bible. Your chance at eternal life in the Kingdom of God has been secured. Don't be deceived. The Angels have already provided all you need to know. The only thing left is to study the Word of God, to keep the Commandments, and to become fully versed and have Faith in the testimony of Jesus Christ.

Summary

The Bible provides the following possible scenario:

After the physical creation of the universe, and particularly the earth with its early life forms, some of the angels thought they had better ideas, and went against the wishes of the Creator. Confrontation with God then leads to open rebellion. After experimenting with earlier ecosystems, God allowed a final life extinction event.

New life were created, and humans that may have had some similarities with an earlier ape species, but with far superior mental capabilities. Of utmost importance was the ability to communicate with God, and His righteous Angels. Humans would experience life in the flesh, and at times suffer pain like the animals. They had to comprehend what the animal kingdom experience, to develop comprehension and compassion. The same humans can also develop to become like the Angels, but this experience on the earth must first prove to them that God is right. They must also have limited life spans so that the damage they do can be limited.

Adam and Eve, our first parents, had a choice, just as the Angels had long ago. They listened to Satan, and that started the current state of affairs of the human race, which would be allowed to continue for six millenniums. However, the righteous Angels, under God's direction, started the salvation process with some humans that understood and decided to worship God and follow His direction.

The honest worship and obedience of Abraham, Isaac and Jacob opened the way to call a whole family that became a nation to a better way in their Promised Land. This was fulfilled in the Exodus. It would be easier to reach out and become more like the righteous Angels when they had freedom to practice Godly religion. Sin among them necessitated the implementation of extra law, particularly the sacrificial law, which should have pained them to the heart, to repent from sin. This was a temporary situation, till Messiah would come to prove worship and obedience in the face of death. He opened the way for many more people to reach out to Angel status. Those that do can be resurrected at the return of Messiah to assist with turning the situation around for the rest of humanity. The earth would become a living paradise, able to sustain the rest of humanity that would be resurrected at the end of the seventh millennium to have a chance to also reach Angel status.

But some sadly believe we are still like the ape species, and can be nothing more. They deny the Creator! Therefor they do not seek Angel status, nor make any effort at studying the scriptures, delivered and inspired by righteous Angels through people of God.

Fortunately there will be a last chance in the second and great resurrection. But sadly they will be underdeveloped compared to the saints, which became like the Angels at the first resurrection, and were part of the most incredible project for a thousand years!

Do those that explain a creation without a Creator thereby discrediting the Bible understand that they could be a stumbling block to billions of people who could become like the Angels?